FOUCAULT

FOR BEGINNERS

WRITERS AND READERS PUBLISHING, INC.

P.O. Box 461, Village Station
New York, NY 10014

c/o Airlift Book Company
26 Eden Grove
London N7 8EF
England

•

Text Copyright: © 1993 Lydia Alix Fillingham
Illustrations: © 1993 Moshe "MOSH" Süsser
Illustrations and Cartooning: Moshe "MOSH" Süsser & George
Cover Illustration: Moshe "MOSH" Süsser
Cover Design: Terrie Dunkelberger
Art Direction & Graphic Book Design: Daryl Long and Terrie Dunkelberger
Production Assistant: Marcia "MONTANA" DeVoe

This book is sold subject to the condition that it shall not, by way of trade or otherwise, be lent, re-sold, hired out, or otherwise circulated without the publisher's prior consent in any form of binding or cover other than that in which it is published and without a similar condition being imposed on the subsequent purchaser.

All rights reserved. No part of this publication may be reproduced, stored in a retrieval system, or transmitted, in any form or by any means, electronic, mechanical, photocopying, recording, or otherwise, without prior permission of the publisher.

A Writers and Readers Documentary Comic Book
Copyright © 1993
Library of Congress Catalog Card Number: 94-060331
ISBN # 0-86316-160-X Trade
1 2 3 4 5 6 7 8 9 0

Manufactured in the United States of America

Beginners Documentary Comic Books are published by Writers and Readers Publishing, Inc. Its trademark, consisting of the words "For Beginners, Writers and Readers Documentary Comic Books" and the Writers and Readers logo, is registered in the U. S. Patent and Trademark Office and in other countries.

FOUCAULT
FOR BEGINNERS

Table of Contents

MICHEL FOUCAULT

INTRODUCTION

First of all, who is this guy, Michel Foucault?

(And how do I pronounce his name?)

Let's answer the second question first.

First name is pronounced like the English girl's name, Michelle. Foucault is **foo** as in fooey, plus **co** as in coco-nut, coming down harder on the coconut.

Who was he?

A French guy, of a peculiar French type,

THE FAMOUS INTELLECTUAL.

The Famous Intellectual of the generation before his was

JEAN-PAUL SARTRE,

who really defined the type: a thinker, with thoughts on a wide variety of subjects, popularly recognized as an important national resource, expected to say brilliant, unexpected things, to get involved in politics from time to time, and to symbolize knowledge and thought for the nation and the world.

After Sartre, there was no agreement about who stood on the intellectual pinnacle.

Struggling towards the peak in the sixties were:

Roland Barthes, the literary critic,

Jacques Lacan, the radical psychiatrist,

Claude Levi-Strauss, the structural anthropologist,

and our own Michel Foucault.

He worked in so many different fields that it is very hard to categorize his work. In a bookstore today you might find his books in Philosophy, History, Psychology, Sociology, Medicine, Gender Studies, and Literary or Cultural Criticism.

What held together his wide field of study was an interest in Power and Knowledge and how they work together.

POWER

KNOWLEDGE

You might say he started with the truism

"KNOWLEDGE IS POWER,"

took it apart, analyzed it, and put it back together. He was particularly interested in Knowledge *of* human beings, and Power that acts *on* human beings.

Suppose we start with the statement

"KNOWLEDGE IS POWER"

but doubt that we have any knowledge of absolute truth.

If you take away the idea of absolute truth, what does knowledge mean?

Maybe knowledge would be just what a group of people get together and decide is true.

But hang on!

According to Foucault, the might of

MIGHT MAKES RIGHT

may not be all that different from the power in

KNOWLEDGE IS POWER.

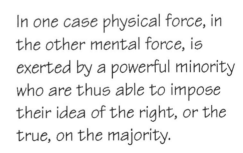

In one case physical force, in the other mental force, is exerted by a powerful minority who are thus able to impose their idea of the right, or the true, on the majority.

When we're talking about knowledge of human beings, the social sciences, or, as Foucault calls them, "the human sciences," then the people deciding what is true (constructing Truth) are deciding matters that define humanity, and affect people in general. If they can get enough people to believe what they have decided, then that may be more important than some unknowable truth.

But hang on!

How do some people get the rest of us to accept their ideas of
who we are? That involves some power to create belief. And
these same people who decide what is knowledge in the first
place can easily claim to be the most knowledgeable—to know
more about us than we do ourselves.

But how does knowledge/power get its work done? Often knowledge/power and physical force are allied, as when a child is spanked to teach her a lesson. But primarily knowledge/power works through language. At a basic level, when a child learns to speak, she picks up the basic knowledge and rules of her culture at the same time.

Take good care of your Mother, Father's off to work.

Daddy work, Mommy stay home.

On a more specialized level, all the human sciences (psychology, sociology, economics, linguistics, even medicine) define human beings at the same time as they describe them, and work together with such institutions as mental hospitals, prisons, factories, schools, and law courts to have specific and serious effects on people.

Foucault focuses throughout his work on a central mechanism of the social sciences—the categorization of people into

NORMAL

&

ABNORMAL

His books study different forms of abnormality:

MADNESS ● ● ● ▶

CRIMINALITY

&

PERVERTED
SEXUALITY.

ILLNESS

We would naturally tend to define

ABNORMAL

as everything which differs significantly
from the

NORMAL

Normal is the basic term, and what is
normal should be perfectly obvious—
it's all around us.

We might also assume that the difference is easy
to tell, and tends to remain the same over time.

But by looking at a wide variety of historical documents, Foucault challenges all of these assumptions. He shows that definitions of madness, illness, criminality, and perverted sexuality vary greatly over time.

Behavior that got people locked up or put in hospitals at one time was glorified in another.

Societies, knowledge/power, and the human sciences have, since the 18th century, carefully defined the difference between normal and abnormal, and then used these definitions all the time to regulate behavior. Distinguishing between the two may appear to be easy, but is in fact extremely difficult—there is always a hazy and highly contested borderline.

Our society has increasingly locked up, excluded, and hidden abnormal people, while nevertheless watching, examining, questioning them carefully.

It has not always been this way. In earlier times madmen were an accepted part of the community; sick people were treated at home; no one expected disabled or disfigured people to stay out of sight; and criminals were punished as publicly as possible.

This exclusion of abnormal people does not make these people unimportant to the culture. The normal is not defined first, with the abnormal established in contrast! We actually define the normal through the abnormal; only through abnormality do we know what normal is. Therefore, although abnormality is excluded and supposedly hidden, the remaining people, normal people, study and question it incessantly, obsessively.

The study of abnormality is one of the main ways that power relations are established in society. When an abnormality and its corresponding norm are defined, somehow it is always the normal person who has power over the abnormal.

The psychologist tells us about the madmen, the physician about the patients, the criminologist (or the legal theorist, or the politician) talks about the criminals, but we never expect to hear the latter talk about the former—what they have to say has already been ruled irrelevant, because by definition they have no knowledge (but that is code for not wanting them to have any power).

Ever-so-quick summary of Foucault's life:

Born in 1926, in Poitiers, a provinicial city, and named Paul-Michel Foucault.

Father Paul was a surgeon, father's father was a surgeon. So guess what Papa wanted young Paul-Michel to be?

When he was 17, Paul-Michel decided he couldn't be a doctor, despite a big fight with his father, and later he decided he

couldn't be Paul, either. When he was 13, World War II began, and Poitiers was occupied by the Germans. In his Jesuit school, Paul-Michel wasn't exactly a war hero, but he did help the other kids steal wood from the Nazis to heat the school.

The war was an ordeal he lived through, but the real adventure of his life was his school career.

The French academic system has, for the most successful students, a sense of competition and excitement about it, probably only equalled in the US by the Olympics.

Foucault entered school, the Lycée Henri-IV, at the age of four. He was too young for school, but he didn't want to be separated from his older sister. For two years he sat in the back of the classroom, playing with crayons, and maybe listening. He liked school, and stayed on, getting top grades in everything but math, until suddenly in his eighth year he was barely passing.

Which just goes to show that you can almost flunk out in junior high and still go on to be one of the greatest minds of your generation, a world-famous Intellectual.

His mother decided it was time for him to go to a Jesuit school, the Collège Saint-Stanislaus. He did very well there, but almost always came in second to his friend Pierre Rivière. (Remember that name, it might come up later.)

Foucault went from school to school, doing extremely well on his exams, until he had reached the summit: he scored fourth among all the students in the country competing for entry to the Ecole Normale Supérieure in Paris—the most exclusive and intellectually intense college-level school in France.

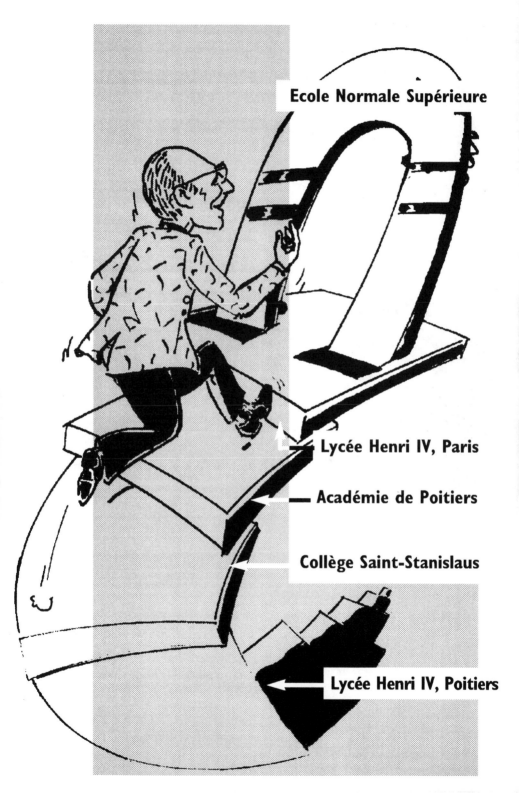

Ecole Normale Supérieure

Lycée Henri IV, Paris

Académie de Poitiers

Collège Saint-Stanislaus

Lycée Henri IV, Poitiers

But at the Ecole Normale, Foucault was not a happy boy. He grew more and more depressed, didn't get along with the others, and finally attempted suicide.

His father took him to see a psychiatrist, whom young Michel told of his sexual interest in men.

Psychiatrists then tended to treat homosexuality as an illness that inevitably caused misery, which didn't do much to relieve Michel's depression.

But he began at this point to get the idea that perhaps psychiatrists were doing more than just helping the distraught—maybe they were mental police, deciding what should or shouldn't be allowed in society.

Still, he wanted to study psychology for himself, and found it fascinating. He read Freud, and the Kinsey Report.

His teachers at the Ecole Normale took students to see patients at a mental hospital in Paris, and to visit another hospital near Orléans for a week each year, to observe both doctors and patients.

Foucault was a bit obsessed with Rorschach tests, giving them to all the students at the Ecole Normale (and to many others throughout his life), and then making quick evaluations of their underlying psyches.

Along with pretty much every one else he knew, Foucault joined the Communist Party (1950-1953), quitting around the time of Stalin's death, when many others were questioning what had been going on in the Soviet Union.

In 1955 Foucault took a job as French instructor in Upsalla, Sweden. There he came upon a huge library of medical works from the 16th to the 20th centuries. For the next few years he immersed himself in this library, and did the research for what would become **Folie et déraison** (**Madness and Civilization**) and **Naissance de la clinique** (**The Birth of the Clinic**).

CIVILIZATION

28

MADNESS & CIVILIZATION

What we have in English is
only a great abridgment of
the original book, which is
over 600 pages long.

Let's begin without any idea of **MADNESS** as completely
separate from, opposite to, reason.

How could that be?
Isn't that what madness is all about, and aren't there
madmen we all recognize?

Well, suppose you see a man who has odd violent outbursts at no one in particular and strikes out at the air around him.

Now you meet another man who tells you that the FBI has planted a radio receiver in his brain and is monitoring his thoughts, and he believes they will soon take control of him. (Let's assume you don't believe him.)

All set, J. Edgar.

Then you meet a man who sits perfectly still and does not move or speak, though you discover that he is physically capable of doing so.

*L*ook at these three men, forgetting for a moment everything you have heard about insanity. Clearly each of them has a problem that may keep him from functioning well in our society.

But would you say that they are all suffering from different versions of the *same disease?*

Would you say that what is wrong with them is their *Reason,* which is broken? Would you think that a similar approach could be taken to cure all three?

Would you say that the one person they are least like is a professor of logic?

They might seem to be using logic very rigorously. If the FBI had placed a transmitter in your brain to monitor your thoughts, it would make sense to suspect them of trying to take control of you.

We might say that they all appear to have emotional problems. But what emotions are specifically involved in any of their actions?

The first two might seem to have problems with their thoughts, but what is the thought-problem of a catatonic man?

Unless you already have the idea of a category such as

MADnESs,

you couldn't think that all these people were the same, and you wouldn't think of them as the opposite of us

REASONABLE

folks. Foucault asks how these categories developed, and how our ideas about ourselves interact with our ideas about the mad.

He starts from the hypothesis that madness has something to do with excluding some people from society, especially by confining them, locking them up.

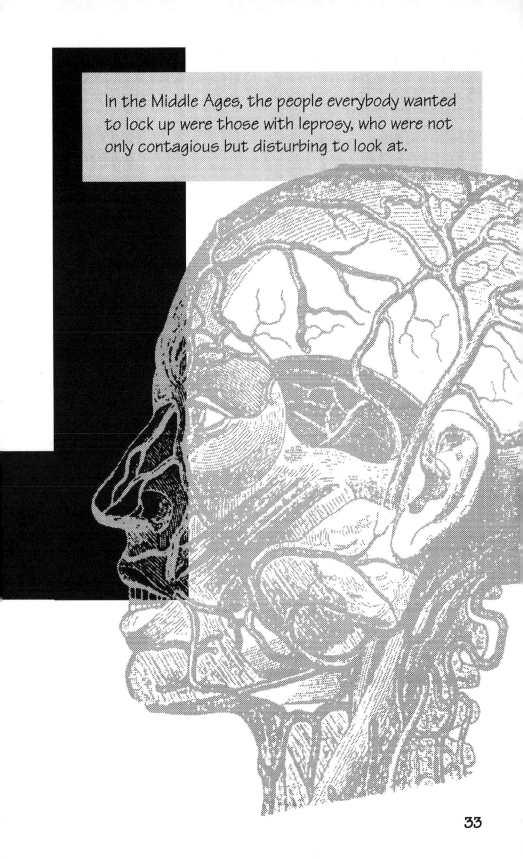

In the Middle Ages, the people everybody wanted to lock up were those with leprosy, who were not only contagious but disturbing to look at.

But then, suddenly, in the 14th century, leprosy disappeared!

Everyone was happy about it, but what were they supposed to do with these big places to lock people up? They left them empty, but just for a while . . .

In the 15th century a new idea cropped up, and became a central image in the popular imagination:

the Ship of Fools.

Wandering down a river, a ship of outcast men are taken from one town to the next, always expelled, frequently with a payment to the captain to keep them on their way.

Why did this image suddenly pop up? A cultural fascination with madness. A terrifying threat that may contain an even more terrifying truth. Erasmus (1466-1536), a Dutch philosopher, wrote **The Praise of Folly** (**Moriae Encomium**, 1509). It and Shakespeare's **King Lear** (1605) both focus on the dangerous insights the madman may have.

"The nature of insanity is surely twofold. One kind is sent from hell by the vengeful furies whenever they let loose their snakes and assail the hearts of men with lust for war, insatiable thirst for gold, the disgrace of forbidden love, parricide, incest. The other is quite different, desirable above everything, and is known to come from me. It occurs whenever some happy mental aberration frees the soul from its anxious cares and at the same time restores it by the addition of manifold delights."

-Folly

Holbein illustration of
The Praise of Folly

King Lear

Thou rascal beadle, hold thy
   bloody hand!
Why dost thou lash that whore?
Strip thine own back,
Thou hotly lusts to use her in
   that kind
For which thou whip'st her.

Through tatter'd
   clothes small vices
   do appear;
Robes and furr'd gowns
   hide all."

The Great Confinement

IN the 17th century, suddenly as many people as possible were locked up. Criminals, yes, for any small infraction, and madmen, anyone acting strangely (and this certainly included epileptics), and the sick who might earlier have been taken care of at home, but the poor as well, anyone out of work. One Parisian in a hundred was confined. This is where the old leprosy houses came in very handy.

GET A JOB OR GO TO JAIL!

The mad became thought of as a subcategory of the unemployed. You might think that the poor were victims of an economic problem, but no, they were creators of a moral one.

Madness was now shameful and must be hidden.

In the 17th and 18th centuries, not content with pinning down the madman, people wanted to pin down the idea of madness as well.

How did they think of madness?

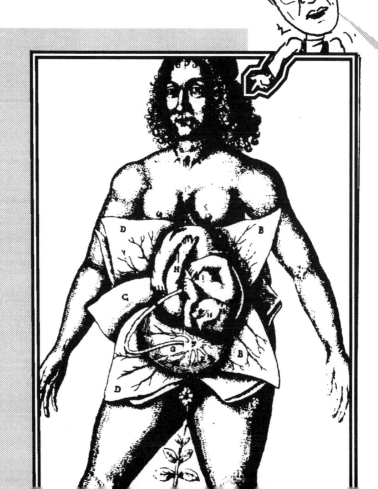

steria

was one of the major ways. At first thought of as a purely physical disease, not grand enough for madness, hysteria was convulsions without any apparent cause.

The word "hysteria" comes from the Greek for womb. Up through the Renaissance it was believed that a woman's uterus could become dislodged from its normal position, and
wander
        about
                the body,
causing
        trouble.

In the 17th century this idea was gradually abandoned, but the idea that hysteria was a woman's problem, and had to do with sex, lingered on.

O h
yes, my dear Michel,
you mention the women in
passing, but you don't say how treatment of hysteria fits in with the treatment of women in general. You don't say
that right through the 19th century
women were frequently locked up as mad
whenever they had sex with someone
they weren't supposed to. And you
don't talk about what happened to
these women when they were
locked up.

By the end of the 18th century, it was said that physical treatment alone would not cure madness.

This did not mark the beginning of psychological treatment,

but rather the breakdown of the unity of body and soul, the breakdown of the internal consistency of the symbol system.

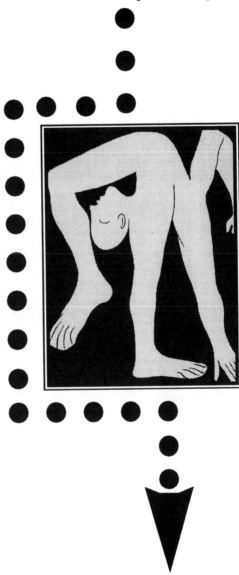

Then out of nowhere came . . .

The French Revolution

M irabeau and the Marquis de Sade, two French Counts were both in prison at the same time, as incorrigible upper-class libertines.

Marquis de Sade   *Mirabeau*

S ade, father of sadism, the "true madman, and truly immoral," is let out first, while Mirabeau, soon to be the hero of his country, rots in jail for no real reason; this irony symbolizes, for the Revolutionaries, the whole problem with the world.

THEN THE REVOLUTION HAPPENS.
STORMING OF THE BASTILLE.
MIRABEAU WILL LEAD THE PEOPLE IN THEIR FIGHT AGAINST

The King

THE PEOPLE ARE IN POWER!
GET RID OF THE KING!
GET RID OF THE CHURCH!
GET RID OF THE RICH!

Until, eventually, too many people are being gotten rid of.

ut meanwhile, this is not quite how the mad experienced it. After the Revolution began, they were supposed to be taken out of prisons (mostly because it was too humiliating to the prisoners to be locked up with them), and put in special hospitals.

But the hospitals didn't exist.
So they were sent home to their families.

Then they were sent away from their homes because they were too much trouble (or at least seemed like they might be).

So they went back into the prisons, but into prisons where madmen and criminals were strictly segregated.

Myths developed of the two great liberators of the mad; noble and wise men who humanized the treatment of insanity:

Pinel (Philippe Pinel), the great liberator of the mad during the French Revolution, walks into the prisons and throws off the chains of the madmen. When questioned, he says, "Citizen, I am convinced that these madmen are so intractable only because they have been deprived of air and liberty."

The mad have their own revolution, and their own liberator.

Samuel Tuke, a gentle Quaker, sets up a rural retreat for the mad. No bars, no chains. Looks like a farm, feels like a family.

The REAL story behind the myth:

Tuke—Yes, the retreat is a family, and the mad are the children, who must learn to respect the authority of the father, Tuke himself. The mad must be raised and disciplined as children. They must be taught religion, the source of all morality, and they must have chores, since work is enormously important in teaching one to regulate oneself. The chains are taken off, but if you are bad, they will be put back on, and you will have only yourself to blame.

As an 18th century mad-man you had a certain kind of freedom from responsibility that was now utterly

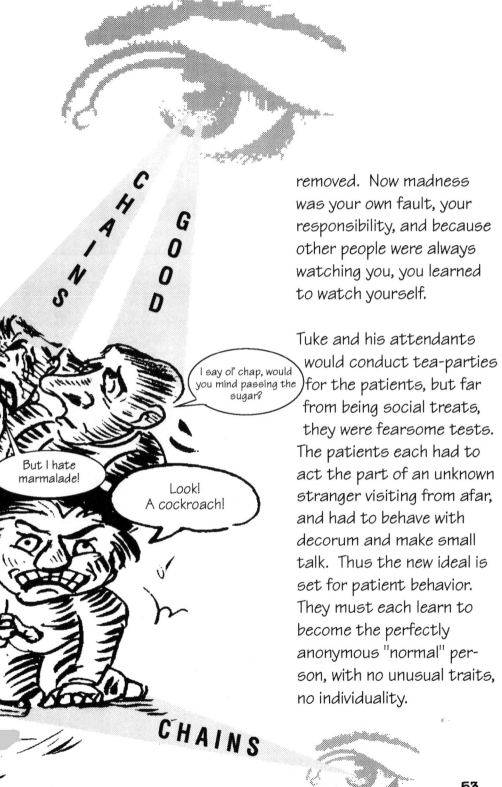

removed. Now madness was your own fault, your responsibility, and because other people were always watching you, you learned to watch yourself.

Tuke and his attendants would conduct tea-parties for the patients, but far from being social treats, they were fearsome tests. The patients each had to act the part of an unknown stranger visiting from afar, and had to behave with decorum and make small talk. Thus the new ideal is set for patient behavior. They must each learn to become the perfectly anonymous "normal" person, with no unusual traits, no individuality.

Pinel established a system of morality very much connected to the newly dominant middle-class as the absolute power within the asylum, and thus the standard for society as a whole. The danger of madness now came from lower-class people who did not wish to conform to this standard.

The keepers continually sat in judgment on the mad, meting out punishment for every transgression.

The pattern of judgment and punishment had to be repeated until firmly **internalized** by the patient.

Enter . . . the Doctor!

(He wasn't there in the older asylums.)

What good can someone trained in medicine do to those who are not physically ill? THE DOCTOR IS A CERTIFIED WISE AND NOBLE MAN. Both Tuke and Pinel found the most important thing to be the presence of a great moral authority, and both hired doctors for their asylums. Gradually the doctor took over as THE FATHER from such non-specialists as Tuke and Pinel. The only problem was that doctors forgot that they were there because they were noble and wise. They thought that medicine was a hard science, that they were in the asylum as scientists, and that they could shed exact light upon this disease.

To the patients, and to the world at large, the doctor's power seemed increasingly magical, even as the doctors told us how scientific it was.

Everything centers on the doctor-patient relationship—only there can the sickness be understood; only there can the cure be effected. And here, at the end of the trail, we find

PAPA FREUD.

Freud knew that the doctor was a wise father, and that it was all about parental authority. Freud knew that the doctor had to be a wise man, and that everything hinged on the doctor-patient relationship—in fact, the cure could be found exactly there—in how the patient reacted to the doctor.

Having been to an analyst himself,
Foucault had some doubts.

Foucault started thinking about Freud
in writing this book, but he wasn't
finished by a long shot.

the
BIRTH
OF THE
CLINIC

THE BIRTH OF THE CLINIC

"This book is about
space,
about language,
and about death;
it is about the act of seeing,
the gaze."

What exactly does Foucault mean by the Clinic?

Actually, you've seen it on TV. Think of Dr. Kildare, Dr. Welby, St. Elsewhere, or Doogie Howser (pick the one from your generation). In all of those shows you've seen the experienced doctor making the rounds of the wards, along with eager and scared novices.

If you've been in a hospital you may have seen the same thing. You probably accept it as a natural part of being sick and in a hospital, part of what helps you. But notice what happens to the patient in these interchanges.

A bunch of people crowd around the bed staring at her, perhaps poking and feeling. She is supposed to be silent unless she is asked a question, and at times she is used as the basis for the ritual humiliation of a student. She becomes a thing, a disease, as the doctors are not interested in anything else about her. (Except, of course, the TV doctor-hero who always sees and understands the real person lying there.)

All of this, the teaching hospital and the notion of clinical medicine as the best method of treating patients and of training doctors, at the same time, is what Foucault refers to by

"LA CLINIQUE."

One big element in its creation was, once again:

The French Revolution

which tended to turn everything on its head.

There were two great medical dreams of the Revolution:

1

● ● ● A nationalized, almost religious order of doctors, who would care for the body as the priests had formerly cared for the soul.

2

● ● ● a perfected social order, with no more disease at all!

The diseases of the poor are products of the horrible conditions in which they live, and the diseases of the rich are the result of their dissipation.

But how do you put such policies into place?

In the Revolution, the first move was to get rid of the old ways. The Universities were seen as the bastions of the elite, so they were done away with. The hospitals were seen as a waste of money—people could be cared for more efficiently at home, within the family. So no more hospitals. Hospital funds were seized, and sometimes saved, sometimes used to fund public charity, and sometimes turned into ready cash.

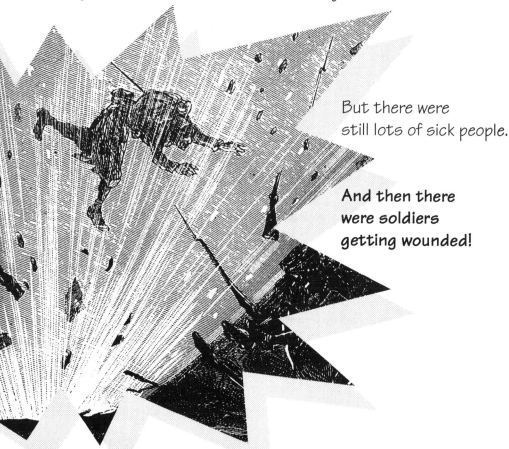

But there were still lots of sick people.

And then there were soldiers getting wounded!

So certainly doctors were needed. Medical officers were needed, and pretty much anyone was accepted and given a little bit of training. These people would return to civilian life as doctors and, unsupervised, could do a lot of damage.

An actual case, from Creuse, that caused several deaths.

"Stomach problems?

We'll have to purge your system, using, um, I guess arsenic would do it.

Didn't work the last few times, but I guess I didn't use enough.

Here, swallow this.**"**

Something had to be done.
University-trained doctors began teaching students in secret.

After the Revolution, the whole system was rebuilt from scratch. Hospitals had to be rebuilt, and they were usually connected to the rebuilt universities.

So what is important about the Clinic?

●● ▶ Teaching is united with practice.

●● ▶ The Clinic becomes a basis for the licensing of doctors, which gradually became much more restricted.

●● ▶ THE PROFESSOR OF MEDICINE becomes a very powerful figure. He examines the patient, and then "examines" the students. At the same time, the professor is always taking a risk. If he makes a blunder, it may be seen by all the students.

●● ▶ Patients accept the clinical rounds as part of their necessary service to the state. Yes, they may die, but nobly, since they will add to human knowledge.

●● ▶ As the place of medical learning, the clinic offers up a series of diseases. All examples of a particular disease may be located in a single ward. The disease is what is important, the individual patient is just an accident. The more unusual the disease, the more interesting the patient. So the diseases are laid out spatially, and the professor walks from one to another, turning his all-powerful eye on each one.

A kind of active vision, what Foucault calls

"the Gaze"

is elevated into
great importance
in medicine.

The doctor's perception is key, and an unobservant doctor is the worst failure. To see all is to be a perfect doctor, where earlier definitions might have stressed the doctor's actions.

"Over all these endeavours on the part of clinical thought to define its methods and scientific norms hovers the great myth of a pure Gaze that would be pure Language: a speaking eye. It would scan the entire hospital field, taking in and gathering together each of the singular events that occurred within it; and as it saw, as it saw ever more and more clearly, it would be turned into speech that states and teaches...."

A desire develops for a complete nosology (a system of classifying all disease) that would be like Linnaeus' taxonomy of plants and animals.

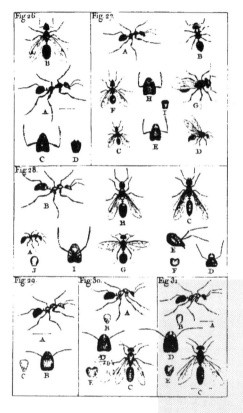

The layout of the hospital wards would match the layout of diseases in the nosology.

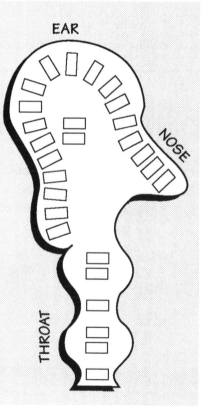

But not enough is known about disease—too much is hidden from the eye. Suddenly there is a new focus:

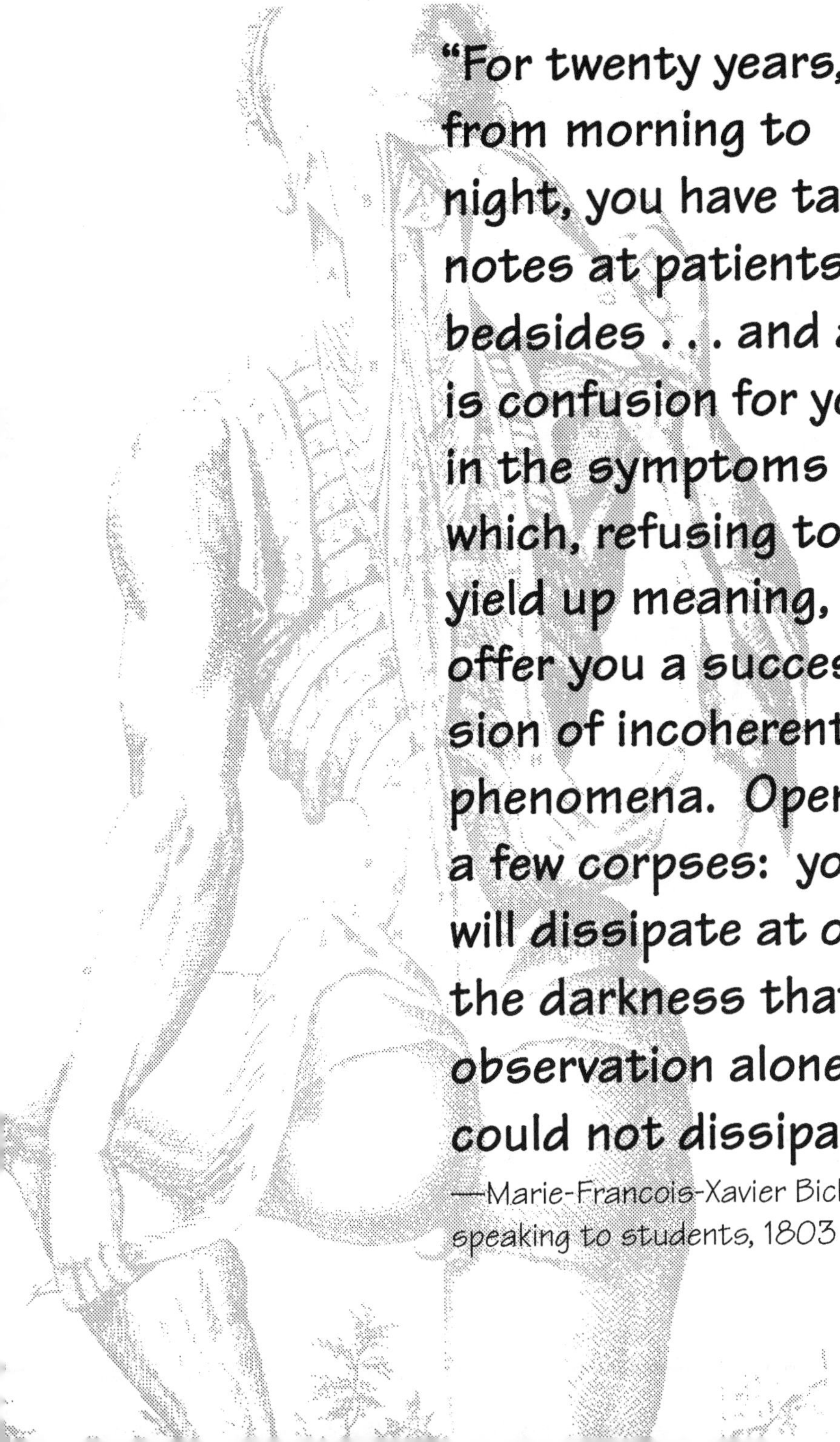

"For twenty years, from morning to night, you have taken notes at patients' bedsides . . . and all is confusion for you in the symptoms which, refusing to yield up meaning, offer you a succession of incoherent phenomena. Open up a few corpses: you will dissipate at once the darkness that observation alone could not dissipate."

—Marie-Francois-Xavier Bichat, speaking to students, 1803

OPEN UP A

FEW CORPSES

Dissecting corpses was not actually so new, but deciding that it was central was very different. Suddenly the eye can see inside the body, and all of disease is visible to the Gaze.

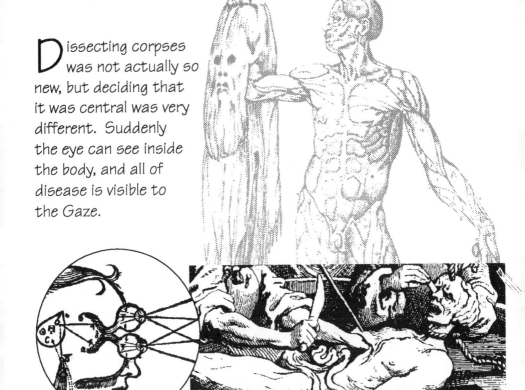

Because this involves the dead body,
the idea of **DEATH** changes.

Death and disease change from purely negative ideas to crucial elements in the process of life.

Death is less the **lack** of life than the **culmination** of life.

And through death, science, at the beginning of the 19th century, begins to take account of the individual.—

a key idea for Foucault.

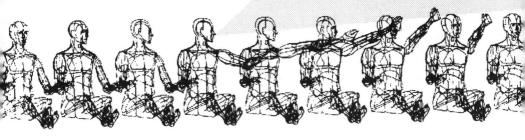

Science focuses on general principles, not on individual circumstances. Newton did not stop his thought at the particular apple that fell on his individual head; he developed a principle that would account for all apples, all objects, falling.

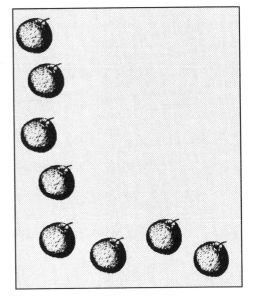

OUCH!

But such science has a great deal of difficulty dealing with human beings. For some reason, we can be very abstract about apples, but when humans are concerned, we tend to care very much about the actual individual.

Around the end of the 18th and the beginning of the 19th centuries, many sciences began to focus on humans, namely the Human Sciences: economics, anthropology, linguistics, psychology and so on.

Medicine is more like **HARD SCIENCE** than the others, but it has always focused on humans. Opening up the corpses, Foucault maintained, gave medicine the opportunity to subject all of the Body to the scientific Gaze.

Thus Scientific Objectivity met the naked individual.

The doctor could look at a person's
outsides
and see the insides,

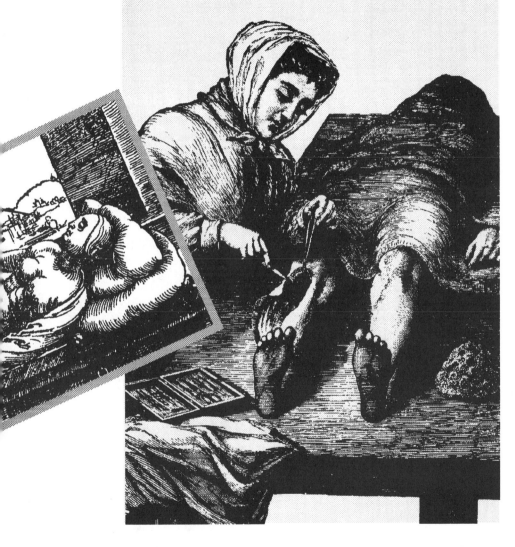

and his power came from his way of
seeing rather than from his abstract
theories.

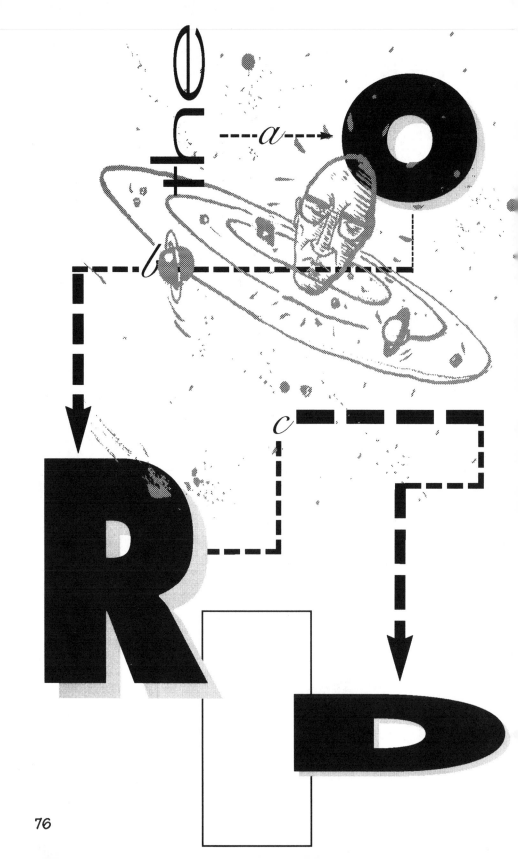

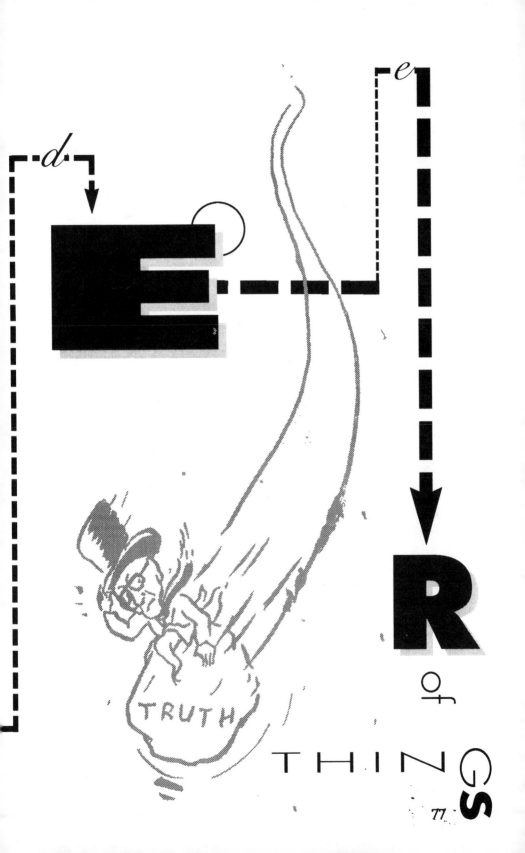

E

d

e

R of

TRUTH

THINGS

In his next book,

The Order of Things,

Foucault looked at the history of the
Human Sciences as a whole.

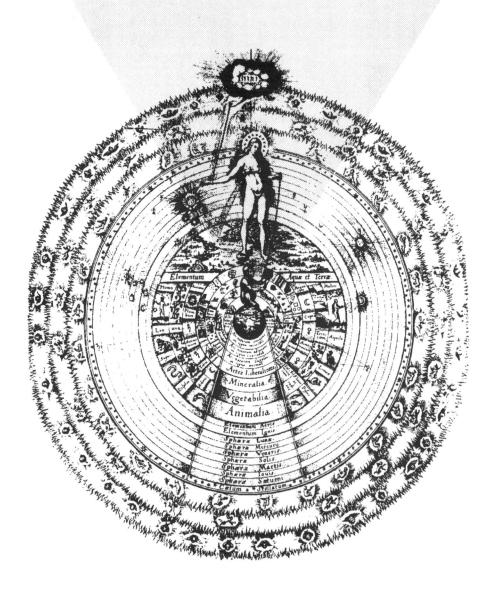

Oddly enough, this enormously complex and difficult book became an immediate hit in France. Suddenly everybody had to have one, and Foucault was famous. He liked the recognition, but suspected that not everyone who bought the book really read and understood it.

As a matter of fact, he always felt that his work was not for everyone. He thought you needed to have a very good background in philosophy and history or his work would just be misunderstood. He wouldn't have approved of this book at all.

A little knowledge is a dangerous thing.

I don't care what he would have thought. I think a little understanding is better than none, and you have to start somewhere.

Foucault starts **The Order of Things** by quoting a passage from the Argentine writer Jorge Luis Borges:

This passage quotes "**a certain Chinese encyclopedia**" in which it is written that "**animals are divided into:**
(a) belonging to the Emperor,
(b) embalmed,
(c) tame,
(d) suckling pigs,
(e) sirens,
(f) fabulous,
(g) stray dogs,
(h) included in the present classification,
(i) frenzied,
(j) innumerable,
(k) drawn with a very fine camelhair brush,
(l) et cetera,
(m) having just broken the water pitcher,
(n) that from a long way off look like flies."

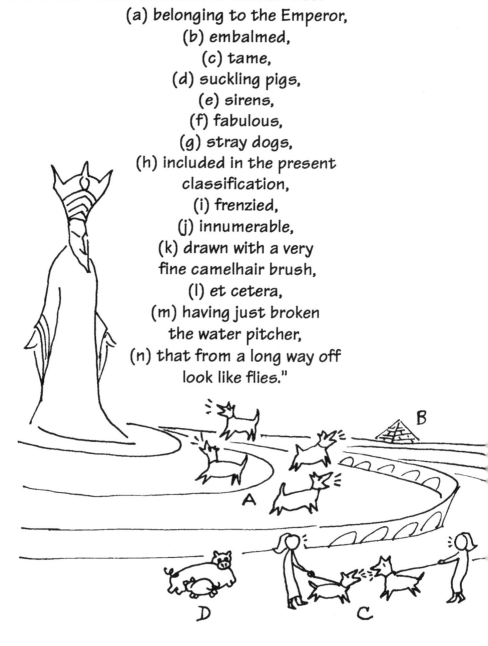

This impossible collection of kinds of animals is so funny to us less because these kinds of animals are all that funny in themselves than because this ridiculous way of categorizing things violates all our sense of order, indeed of the order of things.

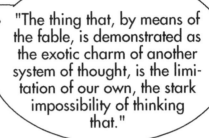

"The thing that, by means of the fable, is demonstrated as the exotic charm of another system of thought, is the limitation of our own, the stark impossibility of thinking that."

We all know when categories make sense and when they don't. Foucault wanted to see what it **is** "we all know," what that knowledge of how to form categories is, and how it would have been different in earlier times.

In *The Order of Things* he examines three major areas of the human sciences,

He looks at the structure of knowledge of a time, its way of establishing order. But he starts long before the existence of the human sciences, and examines the development of the fields known in the 17th and 18th centuries as

What marks the shift into the modern world?
Before the 18th century, Man did not exist.

Now what the **hell** does that mean?

Of course human beings existed before that, and may even have looked at themselves as the center of the universe.

But they were central because God had made them that way. God was necessarily more central, and was the source of all knowledge. Human knowledge was limited, God's was infinite. In the 18th and 19th centuries, God lost his place as the firm center of all, who made all knowledge possible. Man was left with only himself at the center, as the source of knowing, and thus turned to intense examination of what this knowing being was.

The Human Sciences sprang up as old fields were reexamined with a new notion of Man as both the object and the subject of study.

(FOUCAULT DOESN'T EVER COMMENT ON THE MALENESS OF MAN.)

But this modern age will not last forever.

GOD
IS
DEAD

"Man is neither the oldest nor the most constant problem that has been posed for human knowledge."

As Nietzsche had heralded the death of God,
Foucault now predicted a death of Man.

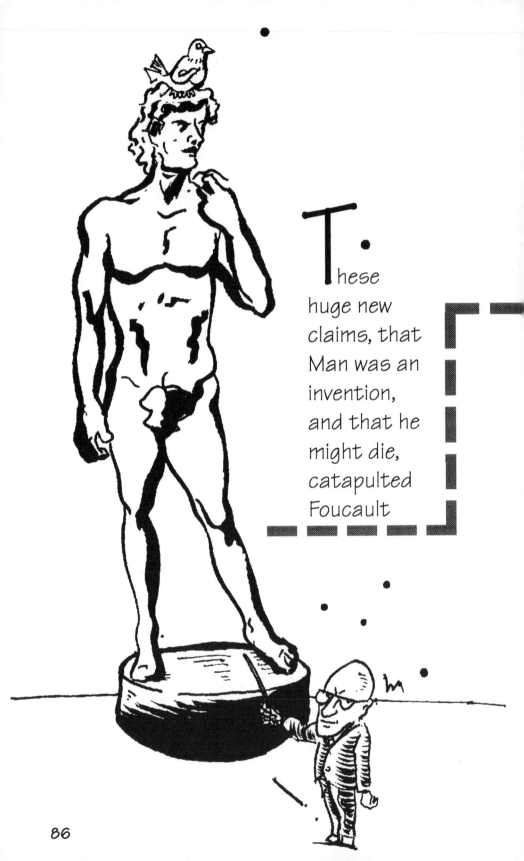

T.

These huge new claims, that Man was an invention, and that he might die, catapulted Foucault into the highly visible forefront of French thought.

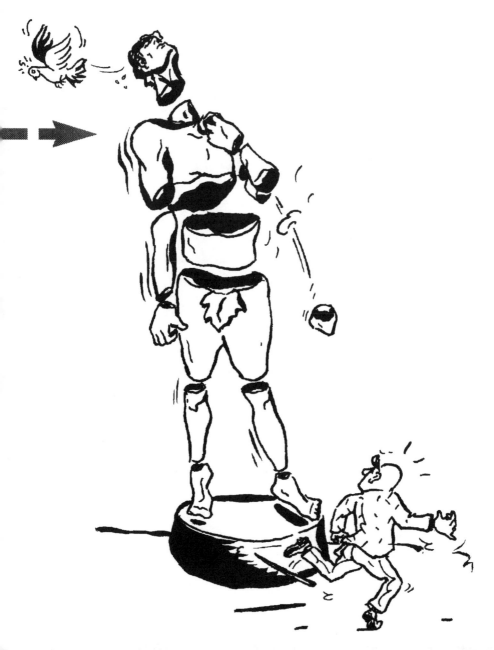

As I said at the beginning, every intellectual of Foucault's generation had to see himself as coming **after Sartre.**

After me!
I wasn't dead yet!
Michel and I marched in
demonstrations together!

Jean-Paul Sartre
(1905-1980)

The Order of Things presented a direct challenge to Sartre's Humanism.

Sartre's autobiography is titled
Les Mots ("Words").

The French title of **The Order of Things** is
Les Mots et les choses
("Words and Things").

What was Foucault challenging?

Sartre's famous dictum, "Existence precedes essence," established the idea that the essence, or meaning of things, was not predetermined by any outside force. Instead, meaning is constructed by **men**. (As Beauvoir would say, "Yes that's right. By men. That's the whole problem.") The world does not contain any transcendent meaning, we make up the meaning as we go along, filtering the world through language.

So far so good. Foucault built on these ideas, as did everyone else around him.

But the problem comes in with Sartre's notion of Existential freedom. **Because** no meaning is predetermined, each person is free to create his own meaning through his own actions. But that freedom itself is a given, something we either have to accept or try to deny or hide from. Any time we do not accept our essential freedom, we are acting in **bad faith**.

Simone de Beauvoir (1908-1986) started to question whether the role of social conditions in limiting freedom might not be more severe than Sartre said it was. Later thinkers agreed with her questions and amplified this doubt.

Aren't people constrained by the ideas presented to them? Aren't you making things a little bit easier than they really are?

Simone, how could you say that? You know I revere as we all do the great philosopher of social conditions, Karl Marx. But I can't help thinking that however oppressed circumstances or other people may render us, we will still have some choices of action or inaction, and we must take full responsibility for those decisions.

I'm not so sure. Take women. As *The Second Sex* (1949) we are brought up in a world defined by men, and we ourselves are defined by men. How free are we to break away from the definition of ourselves as secondary if we never encounter any other definition?

Yes, dear.

The Structuralists

In the post-War period, many intellectu-
als agreed with Beauvoir's doubts about
individual freedom. Emphasizing the
importance of the structures of society
in creating the individual, they became
known collectively as Structuralists.
Foucault was largely counted as a
Structuralist in the mid-sixties.
Who were these people?

They started by resurrecting the work of **Ferdinand de Saussure** (1857-1913), a theorist in the emerging field of linguistics, who had been largely ignored until the 50's and 60's.

In any language, the relationship of **signifier** to **signified** is arbitrary.

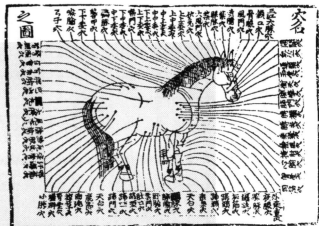

The collection of sounds and letters that make up the word "horse" (the signifier) do not in themselves have any connection to the animal we see cantering about a field (the signified). A "horse" is called, around the world, "cheval" in French, "pferd" in German, "farasi" in Swahili, "hest" in Norwegian, "konj" in Serbo-Croatian, "ceffyl" in Welsh, "at" in Turkish, "caballo" in Spanish, and could just as easily be called a "glymph" in any of these languages (and it still would smell as sweet). The answers to how meaning works lies not in these sounds and letters, but in the whole system of language.

Saussure looked at language as a whole, to see how it worked, rather than focusing on the details of individual languages.

Foucault wrote about such ideas most directly in his short, playful book on the painter Rene Magritte, "C'eci n'est pas une pipe" **(This Is Not a Pipe).**

A

GEORGE   MOSH

"The picture of the pipe is saying, 'You see me so clearly that it would be ridiculous for me to arrange myself so as to write: This is a pipe. To be sure, words would draw me less adequately than I represent myself.' The text in turn prescribes, 'Take me for what I manifestly am—letters placed beside one another, arranged and shaped so as to facilitate reading, assure recognition, and open themselves to even the most stammering schoolboy. I am no more than the words you are now reading.' "

B

Saussure

Back to Structuralism...

"The system of language is a vast structure that is always changing. Before me, linguistics focused on how languages change over time, but that doesn't give you any glimpse of language as a whole. We need to take a snapshot of a language at a particular time, and examine all the rules that hold it together."

The anthropologist **Claude Lévi-Strauss** expanded Saussure's ideas to talk about culture in general. He theorized that within a culture, like a language, all of society, all human relations were governed by certain overarching rules. He studied these rules and found that they centered around certain binary opposi-tions, like up/down, good/bad, and male/female.

Lévi-Strauss and the Structuralists believed that:

•Binary oppositions are paramount.

•The rules binding binary oppositions can best be studied by freezing time and looking at a single moment.

•The structure of language is the dominant one, and that people come into existence through language. Thus one is not "free" to think anything outside the rules of one's language.

So was Michel Foucault a Structuralist? Well, on the one hand, no: he was an historian, and was particularly interested in change over time.

But in other ways, yes. In examining change over time, he hardly avoided structure. His next book, **The Archaeology of Knowledge**, was an explanation of his own aims and methods.

WARNING:

DESPITE BEING AN EXPLANATION OF WHAT HE IS DOING, *ARCHAEOLOGY OF KNOWLEDGE* IS NOT RECOMMENDED AS YOUR FIRST FOUCAULT BOOK. IT IS ONE OF HIS MOST DIFFICULT TO READ (ALONG WITH *THE ORDER OF THINGS*). HE MAKES UP TERMS AS HE GOES ALONG, WITHOUT EXPLAINING THEM, AND HIS LOGIC TWISTS AND TURNS DANGEROUSLY. ALSO, AS AN EXAMINATION OF HIS OVERALL PLAN, IT IS VERY ABSTRACT, WITHOUT THE CONCRETE EXAMPLES THAT ARE SO COMPELLING (AND OFTEN STOMACH-CHURNING) IN HIS OTHER WRITINGS. BRILLIANT, OF COURSE. ANYTHING THIS DIFFICULT MUST BE BRILLIANT.

He named his method Archaeology because of the idea of uncovering layers of civilization. He posits that stability in systems of thought and discourse could exist for relatively long periods, and then change could happen quite suddenly. **The Birth of the Clinic**, for instance, is centered on a change in medical thought and practice at the end of the eighteenth century.

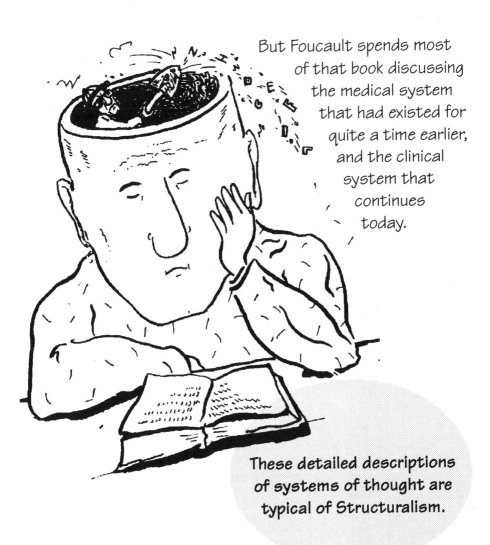

But Foucault spends most of that book discussing the medical system that had existed for quite a time earlier, and the clinical system that continues today.

These detailed descriptions of systems of thought are typical of Structuralism.

Is Foucault a Marxist?

But let's go back to an earlier point, to another thinker who discerns systems that structure society. Sartre told us he was a Marxist. Foucault's whole generation was rebelling against Sartre. Were they therefore rebelling against Marx too? Was Foucault a Marxist or an anti-Marxist?

First of all, what is a Marxist?

Damned if I know. All sorts of people with the strangest ideas have claimed to be my followers.

Marxism consists of two major strands:

1.) An adhesion to Marx's vision of the future, the revolution of the proletariat, and the formation of a new, Marxist state.

2.) An analysis of history based on Marx's economic materialism. History seen as a progression from one economic system, one mode of production, to the next, with all of society and culture determined by the details of the economic structure.

And anyone who doesn't work to unite the strands is no follower of mine.

Nearly every intellectual of Foucault's generation joined the Communist party, embracing the Marxist revolutionary ideal. Structuralists also found Marx's historical analysis congenial because it deemphasized the power of the individual, whom it saw as created by the dominant ideology of the day, which was itself created by the economic system. However, where Marx would claim the economic structure as dominant above all others, the Structuralists would have given language the greater dominance.

Michel Foucault joined the Communist Party later than most of his friends, and dropped out earlier (he was probably an official party member from 1950 to 1953).

It is hard to tell whether he left the party because he suspected some of the atrocities of Stalin, or because Michel did not like to follow the crowd.

F oucault didn't believe in economics as the basis for history. In **Archaeology**, discourse is the source, but it only seems to affect other discourse.

What exactly does "discourse" mean?

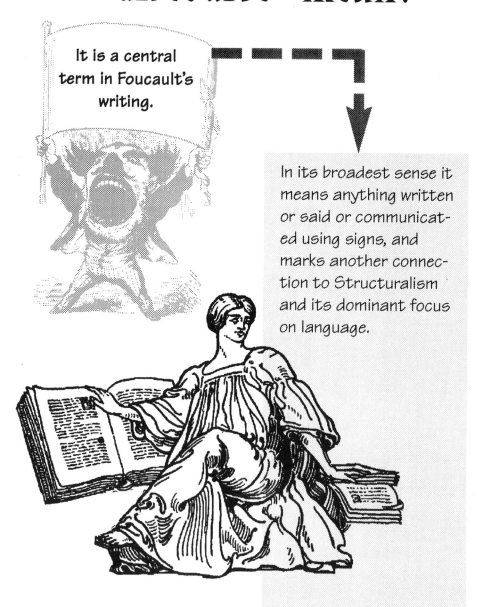

It is a central term in Foucault's writing.

In its broadest sense it means anything written or said or communicated using signs, and marks another connection to Structuralism and its dominant focus on language.

oucault also has a very specific meaning: writings in an area of technical knowledge—that is, areas in which there are specialists, specialized or technical knowledge, and specialized or technical vocabulary.

Each era will define its own discourses, and these definitions may vary radically over time. Take the difference between the field named "Natural History" and the field named "Biology."

The idea is that technical specialists always work together to establish their field and its dominant ideas. These technical fields have had ever-increasing power over people, and these discourses have profoundly shaped the **structure** of our society.

For instance, the discourse on madness, produced by psychiatrists, psychologists, social workers and other Experts define the roles of craziness, and thus also the roles of normalcy that we all take on.

Spare the Rod
&
Spoil the Child

Foucault's model of history shifted after rereading Nietzsche's **Genealogy of Morals**.

Friedrich Nietzsche (1844-1900) was a deep and abiding influence on Foucault, who was particularly interested in Nietzsche's rejection of the notions of rational man and absolute truth, and his founding of history in irrationality and accident.

From the layered model suggested by the term "archaeology," Foucault moved to what he would call "genealogy," which he conceived as a series of infinitely proliferating branches. He began to stress that many branches led nowhere, and that looking for a logic to the progression was misguided.

"To follow the complex course of descent is to identify the accidents, the errors, the false appraisals, and the faulty calculations that gave birth to those things that continue to exist and have value for us; it is to discover that truth or being do not lie at the root of what we know and what we are, but the exteriority of accidents."

This is a drawing from Darwin's notebooks, showing his image of an evolutionary "genealogy," with multiple branches and dead ends, not unified progress towards perfection.

Traditional history's search for origins in great moral truths is entirely misguided; everything is subject to history's disintegrating gaze. There are no absolutes.

"We believe that feelings are immutable, but every sentiment, particularly the noblest and most disinterested, has a history. We believe, in any event, that the body obeys the exclusive laws of physiology and that it escapes the influence of history, but this too is false.

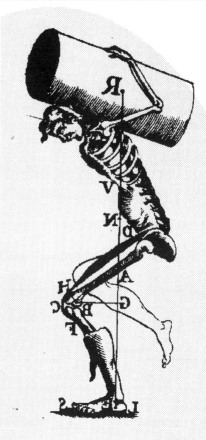

The body is molded by a great many distinct regimes; it is broken down by the rhythms of work, rest, and holidays; it is poisoned by food or values, through eating habits or moral laws; it constructs resistances."

Foucault's life was also changing rapidly in the late 50's and the 60's, as was everyone else's.

Paris in May of 1968 seemed to be in the midst of a violent revolution. Students took over buildings, and were attacked by the police. Leaders of the radical left proclaimed themselves Maoists, and demanded an end to all institutions, all hierarchy.

Where was Foucault in all this uproar?
In Tunisia actually.

From 1954 on, Foucault had taken a series of
teaching jobs away from France — in Sweden,
Poland, and Germany. In 1960 he returned to
France to teach philosophy and psychology at
the University of Clermont-Ferrand.

Then in 1966 he took
a job in Tunisia, in
order to be near his
long-time companion,
Daniel Defert.

He may have missed the May student revolt in Paris, but Tunisia had its own student protest. Communist students rebelled against the repressive, anti-Communist, pro-American government that was trying to modernize Tunisia as rapidly as possible. These protests, unlike those in France, were life-and-death affairs. Students regularly received jail sentences of eight, ten, fourteen years.

vivre libre
ou mourir

Several of Foucault's students were among those arrested. He tried to speak up for them in court, but was not admitted to the secret trials. He helped other students escape arrest by hiding them in his apartment.

When Foucault returned to France in late '68, he was ready for political action. He was named to head the philosophy department in a new campus of the University of Paris. He chose the most radical philosophers he could think of, and tried to hold his whirlwind of a department together until '70.

Then he got one of the most prestigious appoint-ments in the French intel-lectual world: he was elected to the Collège de France. The only duties were to give a series of public lectures on his work-in-progress each year.

He used the freedom and prestige of this position to become politi-cally active in a way that merged his politics and his scholarship.

Together, Daniel Defert and Foucault started a group to investigate and protest prison conditions. But Foucault was also working on a new version of the intellectual as protester.

Sartre had formed the old model:
FAMOUS INTELLECTUAL AS CONSCIENCE OF THE NATION,
bringing his philosophy to bear on important political and moral issues.

Foucault wanted the intellectual to be far less the center of attention. He knew his prestige could get reporters and TV cameras to the prisons, and then he wanted to

SHUT UP

and let the prisoners themselves do the talking.

In '71 and '72 there were a series of prison riots in France. Foucault helped prisoners publish the details of the excessively harsh conditions of their lives.

F oucault was now hard at work researching the history of prisons. Together with his research group of graduate students, he published a collection of documents on a French murder case of 1835. *I, Pierre Riviere, having slaughtered my mother, my sister, and my brother. . . : A Case of Parricide in the 19th Century* contains all the court documents, including a most extraordinary confession, along with brief essays by Foucault and his students in the seminar. Many of the documents address the question of whether Pierre Riviere was crazy, and thus form a bridge between Foucault's work on madness, and his next work.

Foucault's next book (**Discipline and Punish**) moves away from **Archaeology's** abstract Structuralism, and tells a tale of power relations and oppression. His interest in prisons becomes an inquiry into the origins of prisons as a form of punishment. In general his focus will now be on discourse's role in power relations, and how the seeming abstractions of discourse have very concrete material effects on people's bodies.

Discipline & Punish

𝔇iscipline & 𝔓unish

(OR, HOW TO BECOME A CIVILIZED NATION IN LESS THAN A HUNDRED YEARS)

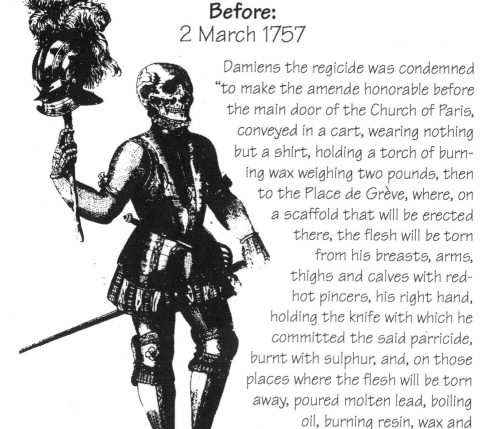

Before:
2 March 1757

Damiens the regicide was condemned "to make the amende honorable before the main door of the Church of Paris, conveyed in a cart, wearing nothing but a shirt, holding a torch of burning wax weighing two pounds, then to the Place de Grève, where, on a scaffold that will be erected there, the flesh will be torn from his breasts, arms, thighs and calves with red-hot pincers, his right hand, holding the knife with which he committed the said parricide, burnt with sulphur, and, on those places where the flesh will be torn away, poured molten lead, boiling oil, burning resin, wax and sulphur melted together and then his body drawn and quartered by four horses and his limbs and body consumed by fire, reduced to ashes, and his ashes thrown to the winds."

(Now I know that sounds gross enough, but the story told by eyewitnesses is far messier. It turns out to be not at all easy to tear flesh off a body with red-hot pincers. The horses which were supposed to pull his body apart by the limbs could not do so, never having had a chance to practice. The executioner's men had to cut the body to pieces, but Damiens' limbless body was still alive when it was thrown on the fire. Ooh, I know, gross, yucchh, did I have to tell you all this? The point is that the intensity of your reaction shows how far we have moved away from the culture that thought this appropriate punishment.)

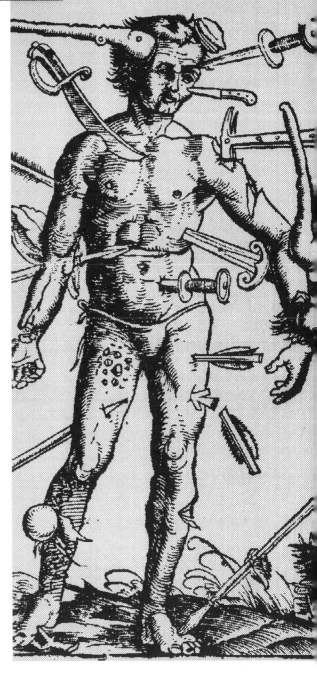

After:
1837

L éon Faucher sets up a schedule for a prison in Paris: "The prisoners' day will begin at six in the morning in winter and at five in summer. They will work for nine hours a day throughout the year. Two hours a day will be devoted to instruction. Work and the day will end at nine o'clock in winter and at eight in summer.

"Rising. At the first drum-roll, the prisoners must rise and dress in silence, as the supervisor opens the cell doors. At the second drum-roll, they must be dressed and make their beds. At the third, they must line up and proceed to the chapel for morning prayer. There is a five-minute interval between each drum roll."

And on and on, so that every second is carefully planned.

No, these two punishments do not apply to the same crime or to the same kind of criminal. But each is the epitome of a method of punishment, and one seems very familiar, while the other is extremely foreign. So what caused the change? You could look at it as the birth of modern culture, or you could say that society had simply become more humane in the intervening years.

Or you could, as Foucault does, look at it as a change in the systematic use of power and authority in a society, and note that the second punishment might not indicate a lesser use of power. Careful control of every aspect of a life can represent a more complete exercise of

power than the massive display of a death.

When we do execute someone now, we take care that it be quick and painless.

Sure, society might kill people, but it wouldn't intentionally cause

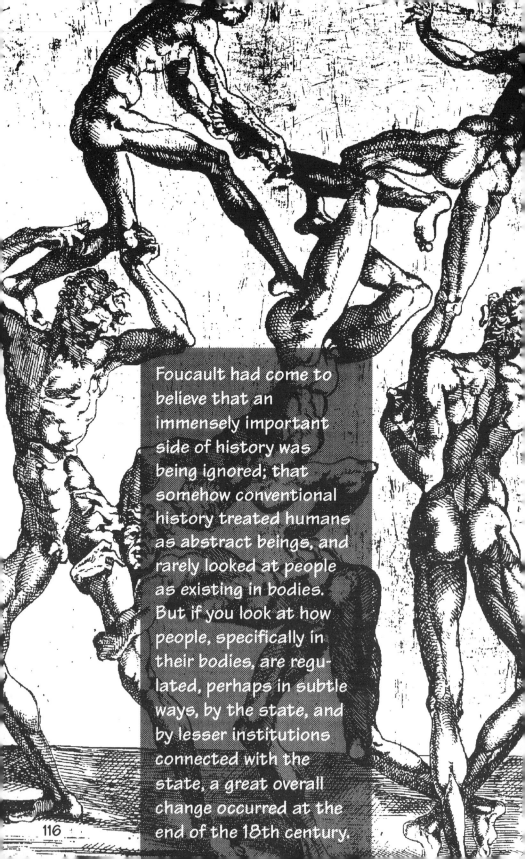

Foucault had come to believe that an immensely important side of history was being ignored; that somehow conventional history treated humans as abstract beings, and rarely looked at people as existing in bodies. But if you look at how people, specifically in their bodies, are regulated, perhaps in subtle ways, by the state, and by lesser institutions connected with the state, a great overall change occurred at the end of the 18th century.

The Importance of Pain

Before, pain was very much a normal part, perhaps the definition, of punishment.

Torture was a crucial part of the trial, & torture during the trial was also part of the punishment.

What? How could the punishment begin before the trial was over? The guy wasn't even guilty yet!

Guilt wasn't viewed then as all or nothing. People weren't simply innocent or guilty, and they certainly weren't innocent until proven guilty. A little proof made a man a little guilty, which might justify a little torture to get a little more evidence. One could not be the object of suspicion and be completely innocent.

After the trial was over, the element of public display was added. Any criminal was a threat to the authority of the king, and the full public regalia of the king's power could be used in a display of vengeance and of order restored.

But during the 18th century, just as philosophers were deciding that the desire to cause pain was not a seemly one for governments, the crowds that came to the spectacles of torture and death became more and more unruly. Something had to be done.

Now we have to switch the scene to outside the penal system, where, meanwhile, a new science of changing—engineering really— the individual develops in the army, schools, hospitals, madhouses, poorhouses, and factories.

Here are its principles:

SPATIALIZATION.

A place for everyone, and everyone in his place. Where someone is indicates who and what he is, as in the wards here, or in schools where the best student moves to the head of the class.

MINUTE CONTROL OF ACTIVITY

(especially using timetables).

"8 to 8:20 will be reading. 8:20 to 8:40, handwriting. 8:40 to 9, spelling; and at 9 there will be a test. Recess is from 9:30 to 9:45, and during that time you will all go out- side and you will **play**."

REPETITIVE EXERCISES.

Must be both standardized and individualized according to rate of progress. Sufficient repetition creates automatic reactions to stimuli...

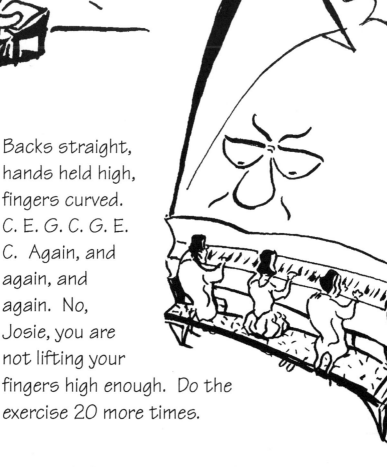

Backs straight, hands held high, fingers curved. C. E. G. C. G. E. C. Again, and again, and again. No, Josie, you are not lifting your fingers high enough. Do the exercise 20 more times.

DETAILED HIERARCHIES

A complex chain of authority and training. Each level of the
hierarchy keeps watch over the lower ranks.

NORMALIZING JUDGMENTS.

That is, a continual analysis of whether the disciplined one deviates in any way from normality. Laws are traditionally set out only in negative terms. They put limits on behavior and decide what is unacceptable. But laws rarely talk about what behavior is desired. As a form of power, the law prevents, but does not specify. Disciplinary power is very different: it not only punishes, it rewards. It gives gold stars for good behavior. And the tendency is for that which transgresses its dictates to be defined not only as bad but as abnormal. It is a more subtle use of power that works on the transgressor from the inside, and consolidates the ranks of the "normal" against all others.

Now you know that is gibberish. You can't go into the open ward until you start making sense.

PRESIDENT'S NEW ECONOMIC PLOICY

Nowhere is the institutionalized use of a concept of normality used as a technique more fully than in a madhouse. Today's madhouses are a series of gradated wards through which the inmate can move only by good, appropriate, sane behavior, as defined by the authorities of the institution.

The innovations of disciplinary power are all brought together in a single architectural innovation.

The Panopticon

"Morals reformed — health preserved — industry invigorated — instruction diffused — public burdens lightened — Economy seated, as it were, upon a rock — the gordian knot of the Poor-Laws not cut, but untied — all by a simple idea in architecture!"

From the Preface to his **Panopticon** by Jeremy Bentham (1748-1832)

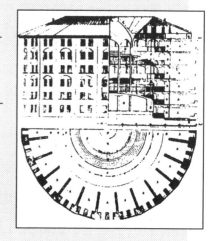

The idea is that every person is isolated in a small room, where they all may be observed at all times by a single person in the center tower. The building would be lit around the perimeter, so that each person could be clearly seen by the central observer, but each inmate would see neither the observer nor any other inmate. Bentham envisioned the same basic concept for factories, schools, barracks, hospitals, madhouses,

and, especially, prisons.

While Discipline was being developed in all these different modes, Punishment was changing as well.

The system centered on pain and spectacle was coming under attack from social theorists, but more important, the spectacles were getting out of hand, becoming a site for political unrest and riots (like the Rodney King riots), and, especially after the French Revolution, great pains were taken to avoid political unrest and riots.

An entire system of carefully articulated and gradated punishments became reduced to a single punishment for all crimes: imprisonment. We are so used to this idea today, it is hard to imagine it as new. But prisons had not been used for punishment, they were simply meant for holding those whose trials were pending, and detaining debtors until they paid off their debts. Many people did not understand the new notion.

Why would putting someone in prison make her a better person?

Why do you want to hide the guilty away? What are you going to do to them?

Put the criminals all together, and they'll just form huge crime networks.

Taking away someone's freedom will not teach him how to act as a free man.

That's punishment? They'll live better than an honest poor man!

These criticisms were heard from the beginning, and they have been heard ever since.

The Panopticon provided a model for using Discipline in prisons. Disciplinary activity became the standard answer to all criticisms. Prisons would necessarily reform the prisoners because Discipline remakes the individual along entirely new lines. Constant observation and penalties for the smallest infraction of the many rules would start the process. Every second of the day and night could be carefully structured. Work, work, and more work, especially of a boring and repetitive nature, would instill proper work habits in the prisoner. As the prisoners became better behaved, they could gradually be granted a whole series of privileges, culminating in a parole based on a careful review of their behavior in prison.

If the prison does succeed in remaking the individual through this process, what kind of person will be made?

A docile worker who does as ordered without question. An automaton, the perfect fodder for the Capitalist factory.

And what about the ones the prison doesn't remake?

The failures?

They come back again and again. Everyone knows that prisons make recidivists.

B ut suppose we take as a premise that if prisons have always had a large number of return inmates, perhaps this very fact is of some advantage to society. What advantage could there possibly be?

Well, the people who become devoted to a life of crime might otherwise be causing worse problems. They might, for instance, go into politics. The prisons are full of petty thieves who steal, again and again, from someone most likely as poor as themselves. Without the prison system as an education in this life, some of these people might generalize about their problems, and theorize on the validity of the very notion of private property. Some of them might organize unions, or riots, or political parties. Instead, those who will not accept the prevailing ideology are systematically channeled into a life story that every penologist knows by heart: the hopeless recidivist, the permanent delinquent.

Or take another prime group of recidivists: prostitutes.

Does society condemn prostitutes, or does it create them? (Trick question. The answer is both.) Are these women rebelling against the role of woman in society, or are they succumbing to it more fully? (Oops, another trick question.) How would one think that a stay in prison would stop a woman from being a prostitute, and why must society be saved from a long series of victimless crimes?

But how does imprisonment help perpetuate women in this role? Prisons help society's criminals network. Prostitutes can form partnerships and locate pimps through prison alliances. They would do so even in the most uncorrupted system. But there is almost always a close relationship between law enforcement and prostitution. In France in the 19th century this relation was formalized. Prostitution was not illegal, but it was illegal to practice it without being on the local cop's register. This cop was a combination health inspector and pimp, and the state was very directly in charge of prostitution.

France in the 19th century and Nevada today are special cases, or are they? The police always decide which prostitutes to arrest, and which to leave alone. They know who has been in prison, and why. They determine the conditions under which prostitution operates, and in many perhaps most cases, paying the police off is the tax a prostitute pays on her tax-free income.

Prostitution is potentially a rebellion against woman's economic, social, and sexual roles. As it mostly works out, however, prostitution is a system run very strictly by men, for men. Female prostitutes are subject to brutal male dominance at every turn.

(Whoa. Did Mr. Foucault say all that? Almost. Almost all of it. He says very clearly that the whole business of prostitution is a direct profit to the state. He didn't quite get around to saying that this potential threat to gender roles is contained by an overemphasis on gender roles. But I'm sure he was just about to. After all, his next book is the one where he really does look at women's issues.)

HISTORY OF SEXUALITY

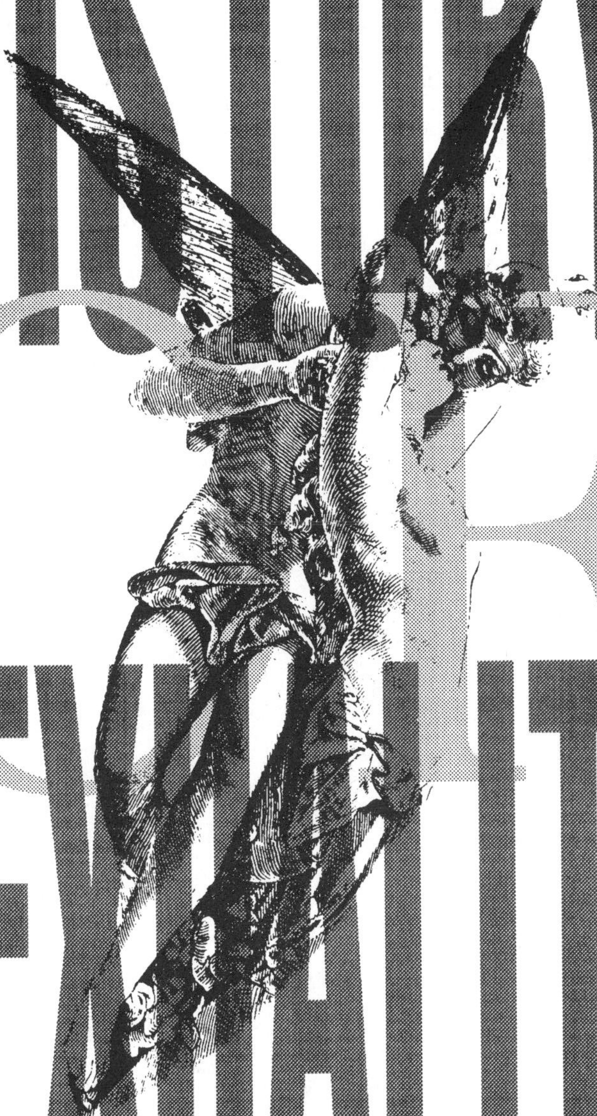

THE HISTORY OF SEXUALITY, VOLUME I

THE REPRESSIVE HYPOTHESIS

Foucault identifies a conventional "enlightened" view of sexuality:

> We all know about the Victorians and sex.

Publicly they were superprudes, pretended sex didn't exist, that people didn't have bodies. This was part, by the way, of their campaign against women. They taught the "proper" women that sex wasn't any fun, and that they should think of something else, like cleaning the kitchen, when their husbands did want to try to procreate.

Meanwhile, out on the streets, there were prostitutes everywhere, because, secretly, the Victorians were absolutely sex-mad. It was all they thought about, all the time, and because they were so repressed, sex got all twisted up for them, and got sicker and sicker.

Queen Victoria was one side of the picture,

Jack the Ripper was the other, and

> they were really the same person!

So what we've needed since then is to be able to talk about sex openly—that's the only way to cure the sickness. Papa Freud was the first person to explain all this, and ever since we've been trying as hard as we can to be honest and open and healthy about sex, to throw away the evil restrictions of the dirty-minded men who control the world. Every time we talk about sex we are heroically throwing off our chains, and the sexual revolution is the first step towards any other revolution.

But once again, Foucault claims there is something wrong with this picture that we are all so ready to accept.

"Briefly, my aim is to examine the case of a society which has been loudly castigating itself for its hypocrisy for more than a century, which speaks verbosely of its own silence, takes great pains to relate in detail the things it does not say, denounces the powers it exercises, and promises to liberate itself from the very laws that have made it function."

He does not doubt that in "everyday speech," talk about sex was restricted. What he primarily maintains is that discourses about sex proliferated. Suddenly sex became an object of scientific study, and of careful regulation by many institutions—schools, barracks, prisons, hospitals, and madhouses, among others. All of these discourses are part of the major Western procedure for producing the truth of sex, for defining sex and its cultural meanings, which he calls a *scientia sexualis*.

Scientific discourse on human sexuality lagged far behind what was known about plant and animal reproduction. Two distinct ways of understanding sex existed simultaneously: a biology of reproduction, which developed in parallel with the other sciences, and a medicine of sexuality, which diverged from all other

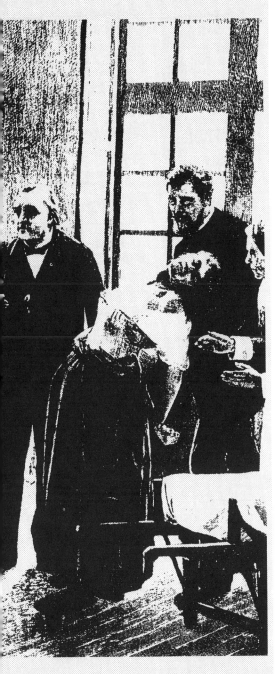

science, went nowhere, nursed bizarre fears, and was distinctly non-rational.

A concrete example of the strangeness of the scientia sexualis is Charcot's work at Salpetriere, the center of French treatment of hysteria in the late 19th century, where Freud got his training. The primarily female patients were put on display for visitors. As Charcot explained each case, the patient would "spontaneously" strike odd, often very sexual poses, which Charcot would describe as "passionate" symptoms of hysteria. A patient's attack could be provoked by a doctor's touching "the region of her ovaries" with a "baton." Perpetually incited to symbolic sexual display, the patients were whisked out of sight if their poses got too specific.

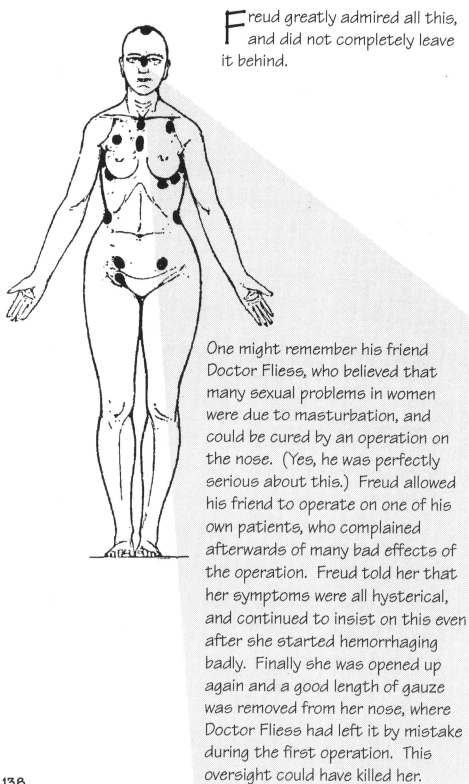

Freud greatly admired all this, and did not completely leave it behind.

One might remember his friend Doctor Fliess, who believed that many sexual problems in women were due to masturbation, and could be cured by an operation on the nose. (Yes, he was perfectly serious about this.) Freud allowed his friend to operate on one of his own patients, who complained afterwards of many bad effects of the operation. Freud told her that her symptoms were all hysterical, and continued to insist on this even after she started hemorrhaging badly. Finally she was opened up again and a good length of gauze was removed from her nose, where Doctor Fliess had left it by mistake during the first operation. This oversight could have killed her.

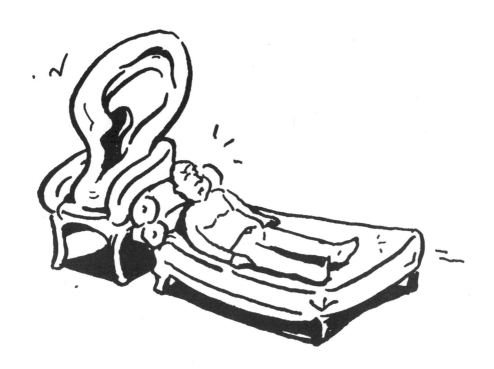

These are just two examples of the medical, scientific knowledge of sex, that already looks to us not just misguided and wrong, but absolutely crazy and perverse. How will our own sexual science look in fifty years?

Such a science of sex developed as a form of power—a psychiatrist somehow has power over a patient simply by sitting and listening.

It is time to undertake a definition of this notion, "power," which is at the heart of so much of my work. Power is "the multiplicity of force relations immanent in the sphere in which they operate and which constitute their own organization." Surely that's clear.

No, not really.

Well then. Take the truism "War is politics pursued by other means," and turn it on its head. "Politics is war pursued by other means." That's true too. Physical force lies unspoken behind many of society's relations. If we don't steal, is it because we know it is wrong, or because we don't want to get beat up in jail? Might be a little bit of both.

It's also true that war and politics are both strategies of power, two methods of persuasion, both in use all the time.

We have a traditional, accepted notion of power within our society.

When you say "traditional," you mean *wrong*, don't you?

Yes. In the traditional notion, power is monolithic, hierarchical, and clearly visible. Power is embodied in the Law, is written down, and is wholly negative, consisting of prohibitions and taboos ("Thou Shalt Not . . ."). That might describe power well enough in a traditional monarchy, but in the last two centuries new methods of power have developed.

"The new methods of power are not ensured by right but by technique, not by law but by normalization, not by punishment but by control, methods that are employed on all levels and in forms that go beyond the state and its apparatus."

As we began to see in **Discipline & Punish**, right and wrong, good and sin, get translated, but only too directly, into normal and pathological.

This new form of power is much more subtle than our traditional notion. It is thus much easier to overlook, and much harder to resist.

SPECIFICATION OF INDIVIDUALS.

"In the Renaissance, sodomy was a category of forbidden acts. . . The 19th century homosexual became a personage, a past, a case history, and a childhood, in addition to being a type of life, a life form, and a morphology, with an indiscreet anatomy and possibly a mysterious physiology. . . . The sodomite had been a temporary aberration; the homosexual was now a species." From this idea we get this book's most striking claim—that the homosexual and homosexuality were invented in the 19th century.

PERPETUAL SPIRALS OF POWER AND PLEASURE.

Penetrating examinations of patients, and pressure on the patient to "confess" all the details, become the way these disciplines operate on people. The examiner and the examinee skirt around each other in a dance. There is pleasure in prying out secrets, pleasure in withholding secrets. And the sites of power in these cases have enormous sexual tension, titillation, built in: shrink & patient, teacher & student, parent & child, priest & penitent.

LOCALIZED POWER. Power is not hierarchical, flowing from the top down, but everywhere local. The president cannot dictate family values (though some of them do try) instead, patterns of power established within families interact with patterns of power in institutions and throughout the social body.

But this idea of power is objected to by many scholars, particularly some historians. They insist that we have to look for "agency." Who are the people exercising this power, creating this system of power? Why are they doing it? Grand schemes are all very well, but history always boils down to individual people doing things. Foucault describes some enormous conspiracy theory, but never tells us who the conspirators could possibly be, or what they got out of it.

I believe this is a very fundamental misinterpretation, but Foucault makes it easy to misinterpret.

"There is no power that is exercised without a series of aims and objectives."

That certainly sounds like someone is carefully plotting and scheming to gain control of people's sexuality.

"But this does not mean that it results from the choice or decision of an individual subject; let us not look for the headquarters that presides over its rationality; neither the cast which governs, nor the groups which control the state apparatus, nor those who make the most important economic decisions direct the entire network of power that functions in a society (and makes it function)."

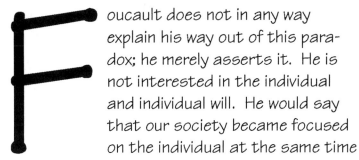

Foucault does not in any way explain his way out of this paradox; he merely asserts it. He is not interested in the individual and individual will. He would say that our society became focused on the individual at the same time that it became a normalizing society, and perhaps the individual, individual rights, is the alibi of power.

**If there is no one in charge of power, no one to blame,
is there any way to resist power?**

Yes, but resistance does not exist outside of the system of power relations. It is, instead, inherently part of the relation. In modern-day normalizing power relations, this tends very much to isolate and individuate resistance into a series of "special cases" which do not allow generalization.

To understand this notion, think of the patients in the back ward of a modern-day mental institution. These people's lives are very tightly controlled. Can they resist? Of course, and they do all the time. But does anyone they see acknowledge that resistance as a rebellion against a power system that has defined them as abnormal and taken control of their lives, that lets them go only if they will live up to society's idea of normality?

I'M **not crazy!** I **don't want to** go to crafts **right now.**

I'm an adult! I can make my own decisions! what gives **YOU** the right to say I'm crazy and **YOU'RE**

not!

Doctors and nurses will hear all of these statements not as political resistance, but as "uncooperative behavior," part of what justifies locking these people up in the first place. Only acceptance of the power system and its terms will get them defined as normal, and thus get them released.

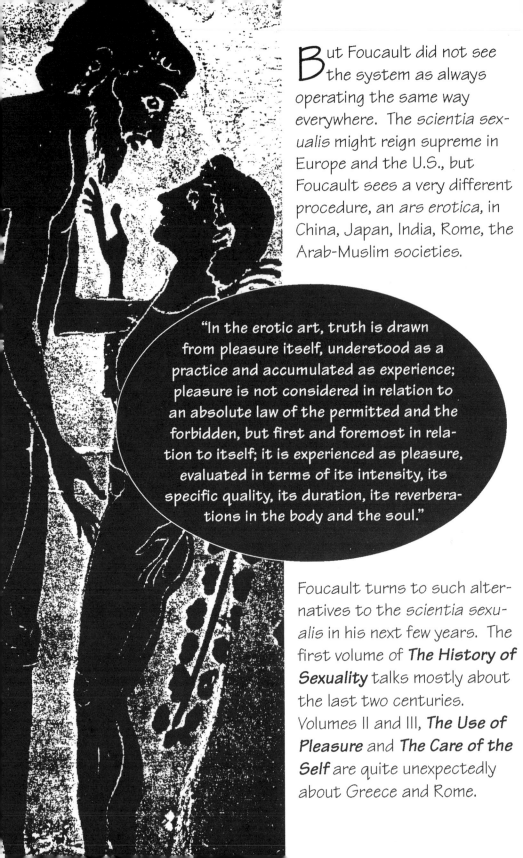

But Foucault did not see the system as always operating the same way everywhere. The *scientia sexualis* might reign supreme in Europe and the U.S., but Foucault sees a very different procedure, an *ars erotica*, in China, Japan, India, Rome, the Arab-Muslim societies.

"In the erotic art, truth is drawn from pleasure itself, understood as a practice and accumulated as experience; pleasure is not considered in relation to an absolute law of the permitted and the forbidden, but first and foremost in relation to itself; it is experienced as pleasure, evaluated in terms of its intensity, its specific quality, its duration, its reverberations in the body and the soul."

Foucault turns to such alternatives to the *scientia sexualis* in his next few years. The first volume of **The History of Sexuality** talks mostly about the last two centuries. Volumes II and III, **The Use of Pleasure** and **The Care of the Self** are quite unexpectedly about Greece and Rome.

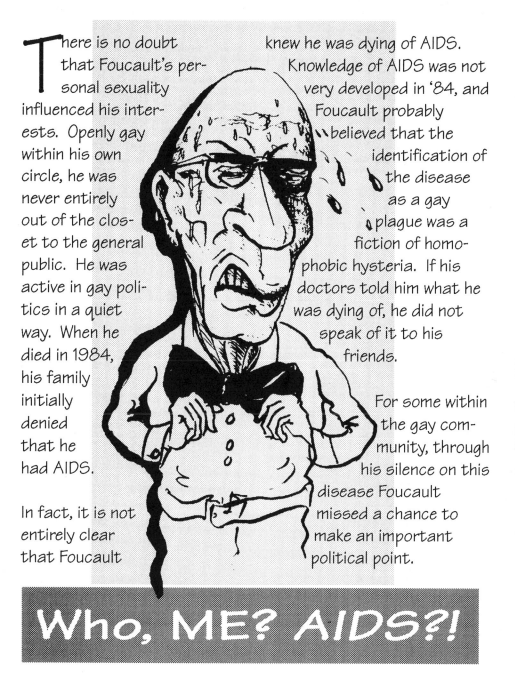

There is no doubt that Foucault's personal sexuality influenced his interests. Openly gay within his own circle, he was never entirely out of the closet to the general public. He was active in gay politics in a quiet way. When he died in 1984, his family initially denied that he had AIDS.

In fact, it is not entirely clear that Foucault knew he was dying of AIDS. Knowledge of AIDS was not very developed in '84, and Foucault probably believed that the identification of the disease as a gay plague was a fiction of homophobic hysteria. If his doctors told him what he was dying of, he did not speak of it to his friends.

For some within the gay community, through his silence on this disease Foucault missed a chance to make an important political point.

Who, ME? AIDS?!

There has also been some controversy surrounding Foucault's involvement in sadomasochism. He enjoyed the leather-bar scene in San Francisco, where some clubs specialize in ritualized forms of sadomasochism known to the community simply as S/M.

Foucault did not believe that involvement in S/M revealed deep subconscious tendencies towards cruelty and violence. Instead he saw S/M as a game, a way of playing and experimenting with the nature of power.

"On this point the S/M game is very interesting because it is a strategic relation, but it is always fluid. Of course there are roles, but everybody knows very well that those roles can be reversed. Sometimes the scene begins with the master and slave, and at the end the slave has become the master. It is an acting out of power structures by a strategic game that is able to give sexual pleasure or bodily pleasure."

S/M was about pleasure for Foucault, but pleasure and politics were never fully separable. This concept of play and transformation helps him solve the trap of being always inside power relations. Scientific discourse may have defined us in terms of our sexuality, and we may be unable to unthink these definitions, to step outside them. Our world may be a back ward we cannot escape. But that does not mean we are simply powerless.

Critics of Foucault maintain that his analysis of power is simply a dead end that disallows any possibility of political action. But Foucault insisted that political resistance was not just possible, but a necessary part of the equation. "You see, if there was no resistance, there would be no power relations, because it would simply be a matter of obedience. So resistance comes first, and resistance remains superior to the forces of the process; power relations are obliged to change with the resistance."

Large political parties and organizations for reform do more to stabilize power relations than to change them. Play, whether sexual or overtly political, challenges society's rules on a deeper and less predictable level, opening up greater possibilities of change.

In 1971 Foucault reflected on the political turmoil of the '60s in terms that reflected his personal life, his politics, and his scholarly work, bringing all these strands together: "We must see our rituals for what they are: completely arbitrary things, tired of games and irony, it is good to be dirty and bearded, to have long hair, to look like a girl when one is a boy (and vice versa); one must put 'in play,' show up, transform, and reverse the systems which quietly order us about. As far as I am concerned, that is what I try to do in my work."

FIN

Further Reading

By Foucault:

Mental Illness and Psychology. Alan Sheridan, trans. New York: Harper & Row, 1976. In French: *Maladie mentale et personnalité,* 1954.

Madness and Civilization: A History of Insanity in the Age of Reason. Richard Howard, trans. New York: Random House, 1965. Abridged version of *Folie et déraison,* 1961.

The Birth of the Clinic: An Archaeology of Medical Perception. A. M. Sheridan Smith, trans. New York: Pantheon, 1973. In French: *Naissance de la clinique: une archéologie du regard médical,* 1963.

Death and the Labyrinth: The World of Raymond Roussel. Charles Raus, trans. Garden City: Doubleday, 1986. In French: *Raymond Roussel,* 1963.

The Order of Things: An Archaeology of the Human Sciences. Alan Sheridan, trans. New York: Pantheon, 1970. In French: *Les Mots et les choses: un archéologie des sciences humaines,* 1966.

The Archaeology of Knowledge. A. M. Sheridan Smith, trans. New York: Pantheon, 1972. In French: *L'archéologie du savior,* 1969.

This is Not a Pipe. James Harkness, trans. Berkeley: University of California Press, 1981. In French: *Ceci n'est pas une pipe: deux lettres et quatre dessins de René Magritte,* 1973.

I, Pierre Riviére, having slaughtered my mother, my sister, and my brother . . . : A Case of Parricide in the 19th Century. Frank Jellinek, trans. Lincoln: University of Nebraska Press, 1975. In French: *Moi, Pierre Rivière, ayant égorgé ma mère, ma soeur et mon frère . . . : un cas de parricide au XIXe siècle,* 1973.

Discipline and Punish: The Birth of the Prison. Alan Sheridan, trans. New York: Pantheon, 1977. In French: *Surveillir et punir: naissance de la prison,* 1975.

The History of Sexuality, Volume I: An Introduction. Robert Hurley, trans. New York: Pantheon, 1977. In French: *Histoire de la sexualité, I: la volonté de savoir,* 1976.

Language, Counter-Memory, Practice: Selected Essays and Interviews. Donald F. Bouchard and Sherry Simon, trans. Ithaca, N.Y.: Cornell University Press, 1977.

Power/Knowledge: Selected Interviews and Other Writings 1972-1977. Colin Gordon, et al., trans. New York: Pantheon, 1980.

The Use of Pleasure, vol. 2 of *The History of Sexuality.* Robert Hurley, trans. New York: Pantheon, 1985. In French: *Histoire de la sexualité, II: l'usage des plaisirs,* 1984.

The Care of the Self, vol. 3 of *The History of Sexuality.* Robert Hurley, trans. New York: Pantheon, 1986. In French: *Histoire de la sexualité, III: le souci de soi,* 1984.

The Foucault Reader. Paul Rabinow, ed. New York: Pantheon, 1984.

The Final Foucault. James Bernauer and David Rasmussen, eds. Cambridge, Mass. : MIT Press, 1987.

Selections. Politics, Philosophy, Culture: Interviews and Other Writings, 1977-1984 . Lawrence D. Kritzman, ed.; Alan Sheridan et al., trans. New York: Routledge, 1988.

Foucault Live: Interviews, 1966-84 . Sylvère Lotringer, ed.; John Johnston, trans. New York: Semiotext(e), 1989.

Remarks on Marx: Conversations with Duccio Trombadori. R. James Goldstein and James Cascaito, eds. New York: Semiotext(e), 1991.

About Foucault:

Baudrillard, Jean. Forget Foucault. New York: Semiotext(e), 1987.

Cooper, Barry. Michel Foucault, an Introduction to the Study of his Thought. New York: Edwin Mellen Press, 1981.

Cousins, Mark. Michel Foucault. New York: St. Martin's Press, 1984.

Deleuze, Gilles. Foucault. Sean Hand, trans. Minneapolis: University of Minnesota Press, 1988.

Dreyfus, Hubert L. and Paul Rabinow. Michel Foucault: Beyond Structuralism and Hermeneutics. With an afterword by and an interview with Michel Foucault. 2nd ed. Chicago: University of Chicago Press, 1983.

During, Simon. Foucault and Literature: Towards a Genealogy of Writing. London: Routledge, 1992.

McNay, Lois. Foucault and Feminism: Power, Gender and the Self. Cambridge: Polity Press, 1992.

Poster, Mark. Foucault, Marxism and History: Mode of Production versus Mode of Information. Cambridge: Polity Press, 1984.

Sawicki, Jana, Disciplining Foucault: Feminism, Power, and the Body. New York: Routledge, 1991.

Sheridan, Alan. Michel Foucault: The Will to Truth. London: Tavistock, 1980.

Shumway, David R. Michel Foucault. Charlottesville: University Press of Virginia, 1992.

Smart, Barry, Michel Foucault. London: Routledge, 1988.

Biographies:

Eribon, Didier. *Michel Foucault.* Betsy Wing, trans. Cambridge, Mass.: Harvard University Press, 1991. A comprehensive biography.

Miller, James. *The Passion of Michel Foucault.* New York: Simon & Schuster, 1993. A biography focusing on the interaction of Foucault's thought and his sexuality.

Collections of Essays:

Arac, Jonathan, ed. *After Foucault: Humanistic Knowledge, Postmodern Challenges.* New Brunswick: Rutgers University Press, 1991.

Caputo, John and Mark Yount, eds. *Foucault and the Critique of Institutions.* University Park, Pa.: Pennsylvania State University Press, 1993.

Diamond, Irene, and Lee Quinby, eds. *Feminism & Foucault: Reflections on Resistance.* Boston: Northeastern University Press, 1988.

Gane, Mike and Terry Johnson, eds. *Foucault's New Domains.* London: Routledge, 1993.

Hoy, David Couzens, ed. *Foucault: A Critical Reader.* Oxford: B. Blackwell, 1986.

Morris, Meaghan and Paul Patton, eds. *Michel Foucault: Power, Truth, Strategy.* Sydney, Australia: Feral Publications, 1979.

Ramazanoglu, Caroline, ed. *Up Against Foucault: Explorations of Some Tensions between Foucault and Feminism.* London: Routledge, 1993.

Index